EMMANUEL JOSEPH

The Rhythm of Enough, Daily Practices for Balance, Growth, and Meaningful Bonds

Copyright © 2025 by Emmanuel Joseph

All rights reserved. No part of this publication may be reproduced, stored or transmitted in any form or by any means, electronic, mechanical, photocopying, recording, scanning, or otherwise without written permission from the publisher. It is illegal to copy this book, post it to a website, or distribute it by any other means without permission.

First edition

This book was professionally typeset on Reedsy.
Find out more at reedsy.com

Contents

1	Chapter 1: The Morning Ritual	1
2	Chapter 2: Embracing Mindfulness	2
3	Chapter 3: Nourishing the Body	3
4	Chapter 4: Cultivating a Growth Mindset	5
5	Chapter 5: Building Meaningful Connections	7
6	Chapter 6: Embracing Simplicity	9
7	Chapter 7: Practicing Gratitude	11
8	Chapter 8: Embracing Creativity	13
9	Chapter 9: The Power of Play	15
10	Chapter 10: The Art of Letting Go	16
11	Chapter 11: The Power of Rest	17
12	Chapter 12: Nurturing Your Passions	18
13	Chapter 13: Finding Joy in the Journey	19
14	Chapter 14: Building a Support Network	20
15	Chapter 15: The Practice of Self-Compassion	21
16	Chapter 16: Living with Intention	22

1

Chapter 1: The Morning Ritual

The sunrise brings with it a sense of possibility and renewal. Each morning, dedicate time to a ritual that grounds you—whether it's meditation, stretching, or a quiet cup of coffee. This practice of stillness allows you to reconnect with yourself before the day's demands take hold. It's in these moments of solitude that clarity and intention find their place.

Creating a morning ritual is not just about the activity, but the consistency. The brain thrives on routine, finding comfort in the familiar. As you repeat these actions each day, you cultivate a sense of stability and peace. This foundation serves as your anchor, helping you navigate the challenges that lie ahead.

Incorporate elements that engage all your senses. The aroma of fresh coffee, the warmth of the rising sun, the sound of birds chirping—each sensory experience enhances your presence in the moment. This holistic approach to your morning ritual enriches your overall well-being, setting a positive tone for the day.

Lastly, use this time to set intentions. Reflect on your goals and aspirations, and visualize the steps you'll take to achieve them. By aligning your actions with your values, you create a sense of purpose that propels you forward with confidence and determination.

2

Chapter 2: Embracing Mindfulness

Mindfulness is the art of living fully in the present moment. It's about being aware of your thoughts, feelings, and surroundings without judgment. This practice cultivates a deeper connection with yourself and the world around you. By embracing mindfulness, you create a space where stress and anxiety have little room to thrive.

Begin by incorporating mindfulness into your daily routine. Simple activities like washing dishes or walking can become moments of mindfulness. Focus on the sensations, the movement, and the experience itself. This conscious awareness transforms mundane tasks into opportunities for reflection and tranquility.

Mindfulness also extends to your interactions with others. Listen actively and empathetically, giving your full attention to the conversation. This level of engagement fosters meaningful connections and strengthens relationships. When you're fully present, you honor the person you're with, creating an environment of mutual respect and understanding.

Mindfulness is not a destination but a journey. It requires patience and practice, but the rewards are profound. As you cultivate this skill, you'll find greater peace, resilience, and clarity. Embrace the journey, and let mindfulness guide you towards a more balanced and fulfilling life.

3

Chapter 3: Nourishing the Body

Our bodies are temples that deserve care and respect. Nourishing the body involves more than just feeding it; it's about providing the nutrients, exercise, and rest it needs to thrive. This holistic approach to health fosters a sense of vitality and well-being that permeates every aspect of life.

Start with your diet. Focus on whole, unprocessed foods that provide the essential vitamins and minerals your body craves. Incorporate a variety of fruits, vegetables, lean proteins, and healthy fats into your meals. By choosing nutrient-dense foods, you fuel your body for optimal performance and longevity.

Physical activity is equally important. Find an exercise routine that you enjoy, whether it's yoga, running, or dancing. Consistency is key, so choose activities that you look forward to. Regular exercise boosts your mood, strengthens your body, and enhances your overall health. It's a powerful tool for maintaining balance and energy.

Rest is the third pillar of a healthy body. Prioritize sleep and relaxation, allowing your body to recover and rejuvenate. Establish a bedtime routine that promotes restful sleep, and create an environment conducive to relaxation. Quality sleep is essential for cognitive function, emotional stability, and physical health.

By nourishing your body with mindful eating, regular exercise, and restful sleep, you create a foundation for a vibrant and healthy life. These practices enhance your physical, mental, and emotional well-being, empowering you to live with vitality and joy.

4

Chapter 4: Cultivating a Growth Mindset

A growth mindset is the belief that abilities and intelligence can be developed through dedication and hard work. This perspective fosters resilience, creativity, and a love of learning. By embracing a growth mindset, you open yourself to new possibilities and experiences, paving the way for personal and professional growth.

Start by challenging your self-limiting beliefs. Recognize that failure is not a reflection of your worth, but an opportunity for growth. Embrace setbacks as learning experiences, and use them to refine your skills and strategies. This shift in perspective empowers you to take risks and pursue your goals with confidence.

Cultivate curiosity and a love of learning. Approach new challenges with an open mind and a willingness to explore. Seek out opportunities for personal and professional development, whether it's through formal education, workshops, or self-directed learning. This continuous pursuit of knowledge enriches your life and broadens your horizons.

Surround yourself with positive influences. Seek out mentors, peers, and communities that support your growth and encourage your aspirations. These relationships provide valuable insights, guidance, and inspiration. By surrounding yourself with individuals who share your values and goals, you create a supportive network that fosters mutual growth and success.

Finally, practice self-compassion. Acknowledge your efforts and celebrate your achievements, no matter how small. Recognize that growth is a journey, and be patient with yourself along the way. By nurturing a growth mindset, you cultivate resilience, creativity, and a sense of purpose that drives you towards your fullest potential.

5

Chapter 5: Building Meaningful Connections

Human connection is at the heart of a fulfilling life. Building meaningful relationships involves more than just socializing; it's about creating bonds that nourish the soul and provide support, love, and understanding. By prioritizing authentic connections, you enrich your life and the lives of those around you.

Begin by fostering genuine communication. Share your thoughts, feelings, and experiences openly and honestly. Practice active listening, showing empathy and understanding towards others. This level of communication builds trust and deepens your connections, creating a foundation for lasting relationships.

Invest time and effort in nurturing your relationships. Schedule regular catch-ups with friends and family, and make an effort to stay connected. Show appreciation and gratitude for the people in your life, and celebrate their achievements and milestones. By investing in your relationships, you demonstrate that you value and care for the people who matter most.

Be present in your interactions. Put away distractions and focus on the person you're with. This presence shows that you value their company and creates a space for meaningful connection. Whether it's a heartfelt conversation or a shared activity, being fully present strengthens your bonds and enhances your relationships.

Finally, practice kindness and compassion. Small acts of kindness can have a profound impact on your relationships. Offer support, lend a helping hand, or simply show that you care. By cultivating a spirit of kindness and compassion, you create a positive and nurturing environment for your relationships to thrive.

6

Chapter 6: Embracing Simplicity

In a world of constant noise and clutter, simplicity offers a path to peace and clarity. Embracing simplicity involves paring down to the essentials and focusing on what truly matters. This minimalist approach to life fosters a sense of balance and contentment, allowing you to live with intention and purpose.

Start by decluttering your physical space. Clear out items that no longer serve a purpose or bring you joy. Create an environment that reflects your values and supports your well-being. This physical simplicity reduces stress and creates a sense of order and harmony in your surroundings.

Simplify your commitments. Evaluate your schedule and prioritize activities that align with your values and goals. Learn to say no to obligations that drain your energy and time. By focusing on what truly matters, you create space for the things that bring you joy and fulfillment.

Embrace simplicity in your thoughts and emotions. Let go of negative self-talk and focus on positive and constructive thoughts. Practice mindfulness and meditation to quiet your mind and cultivate inner peace. This mental simplicity fosters clarity and resilience, allowing you to navigate life with ease and grace.

Finally, simplify your relationships. Surround yourself with people who uplift and support you. Let go of toxic relationships that drain your energy and well-being. By cultivating meaningful connections, you create a network of support and love that enriches your life.

7

Chapter 7: Practicing Gratitude

Gratitude is a powerful practice that shifts your focus from what you lack to what you have. By appreciating the abundance in your life, you cultivate a sense of contentment and joy. Practicing gratitude transforms your perspective, fostering a positive and resilient mindset.

Start by keeping a gratitude journal. Each day, write down three things you're grateful for. These can be simple pleasures, significant achievements, or acts of kindness. This daily practice trains your mind to seek out the positive aspects of your life, enhancing your overall well-being.

Express gratitude to others. Take the time to acknowledge and appreciate the people in your life. Write thank-you notes, send messages of appreciation, or simply express your gratitude in person. This practice strengthens your relationships and creates a ripple effect of positivity.

Incorporate gratitude into your daily routine. Take a moment each morning to reflect on the blessings in your life. Throughout the day, pause to appreciate the beauty around you, the kindness of others, and the opportunities you have. This constant awareness of gratitude fosters a sense of abundance and joy.

Practice gratitude even in challenging times. Recognize the lessons and growth that come from adversity. Find silver linings and appreciate the strength and resilience you've gained. By embracing gratitude in all circumstances, you cultivate a positive and resilient mindset that supports your overall well-being.

8

Chapter 8: Embracing Creativity

Creativity is a powerful force that brings joy, inspiration, and innovation to our lives. Embracing creativity involves making space for imagination, exploration, and self-expression. This practice fosters a sense of fulfillment and personal growth, allowing you to tap into your unique talents and passions.

Start by setting aside dedicated time for creative pursuits. Whether it's painting, writing, music, or any other form of artistic expression, make it a regular part of your routine. This intentional practice nurtures your creativity and allows you to explore new ideas and possibilities.

Create an environment that inspires creativity. Surround yourself with colors, textures, and objects that spark your imagination. Keep a journal or sketchbook to capture your ideas and inspirations. This creative space becomes a sanctuary where you can freely express yourself and explore your artistic vision.

Experiment with different mediums and techniques. Step out of your comfort zone and try new things. Embrace the process of creation, rather than focusing solely on the outcome. This playful and open-minded approach allows you to discover new talents and develop your skills.

Share your creativity with others. Whether it's through collaborations, exhibitions, or simply sharing your work with friends and family, let your creativity shine. This sharing fosters a sense of connection and community, and it allows you to inspire and be inspired by others.

9

Chapter 9: The Power of Play

Play is an essential aspect of a balanced and fulfilling life. It brings joy, relaxation, and a sense of wonder. Embracing play involves making time for fun and leisure, allowing yourself to let go of responsibilities and immerse in activities that bring you joy.

Incorporate play into your daily routine. Set aside time each day for activities that bring you joy and relaxation. This can be anything from playing games, engaging in hobbies, or simply spending time outdoors. This intentional practice of play rejuvenates your mind and body, fostering a sense of balance and well-being.

Embrace a playful mindset. Approach life with curiosity and a sense of adventure. Look for opportunities to infuse fun and creativity into your daily activities. This playful perspective fosters a positive and resilient mindset, allowing you to navigate life's challenges with ease and grace.

Engage in social play. Spend time with friends and family, and participate in activities that bring you closer. Whether it's a game night, a sports event, or simply sharing laughter and stories, social play strengthens your bonds and enhances your relationships.

Allow yourself to be spontaneous. Let go of rigid schedules and expectations, and embrace the joy of the unexpected. This spontaneity brings excitement and novelty to your life, fostering a sense of wonder and discovery.

10

Chapter 10: The Art of Letting Go

Letting go is a powerful practice that brings peace and clarity to our lives. It involves releasing the things that no longer serve us—whether it's physical possessions, negative emotions, or limiting beliefs. By letting go, we create space for new possibilities and experiences, fostering a sense of freedom and growth.

Start by decluttering your physical space. Let go of items that no longer bring you joy or serve a purpose. This physical release creates a sense of order and harmony, allowing you to focus on what truly matters.

Release negative emotions and limiting beliefs. Practice mindfulness and self-reflection to identify the thoughts and feelings that hold you back. Use techniques like journaling, meditation, or therapy to process and let go of these emotions. This emotional release fosters a sense of peace and resilience.

Practice forgiveness. Let go of grudges and resentment, and embrace compassion and understanding. Forgiveness is a powerful act of self-care, allowing you to release the burden of negative emotions and move forward with a light heart.

Embrace change and uncertainty. Let go of the need for control and certainty, and trust in the journey. This acceptance fosters a sense of freedom and openness, allowing you to navigate life with grace and ease.

11

Chapter 11: The Power of Rest

Rest is a vital aspect of a balanced and fulfilling life. It allows our bodies and minds to recover, rejuvenate, and thrive. Embracing rest involves prioritizing sleep, relaxation, and self-care, fostering a sense of well-being and vitality.

Start by prioritizing quality sleep. Establish a bedtime routine that promotes restful sleep. Create an environment conducive to relaxation, free from distractions and stress. Quality sleep is essential for cognitive function, emotional stability, and physical health.

Incorporate relaxation into your daily routine. Set aside time each day for activities that bring you peace and calm. Whether it's reading, meditating, or simply taking a walk in nature, this intentional practice of relaxation rejuvenates your mind and body.

Practice self-care. Take time to nurture yourself, whether it's through a warm bath, a massage, or simply spending time doing something you love. This self-care fosters a sense of well-being and balance, allowing you to recharge and thrive.

Listen to your body. Pay attention to its signals and needs, and give yourself permission to rest when needed. This practice of self-awareness and self-compassion fosters a sense of resilience and vitality, allowing you to navigate life with energy and grace.

12

Chapter 12: Nurturing Your Passions

Passions are the fuel that ignites our souls and brings meaning to our lives. Nurturing your passions involves making time for the activities and interests that bring you joy and fulfillment. This practice fosters a sense of purpose and growth, allowing you to live with intention and enthusiasm.

Identify your passions. Reflect on the activities and interests that bring you joy and fulfillment. Consider what makes you lose track of time or brings a sense of excitement and curiosity. These are the passions that deserve your attention and energy.

Make time for your passions. Incorporate these activities into your daily or weekly routine. Whether it's a hobby, a creative pursuit, or a professional interest, make it a priority. This intentional practice of nurturing your passions fosters a sense of purpose and joy.

Share your passions with others. Engage in communities or groups that share your interests. Whether it's through social media, clubs, or local events, connecting with like-minded individuals fosters a sense of belonging and inspiration.

Pursue personal growth. Continuously seek opportunities to develop your skills and knowledge in your areas of passion. Whether it's through formal education, workshops, or self-directed learning, this pursuit of growth enriches your life and broadens your horizons.

13

Chapter 13: Finding Joy in the Journey

Life is a journey filled with ups and downs, twists and turns. Finding joy in the journey involves embracing each moment with gratitude, curiosity, and a sense of adventure. This practice fosters a positive and resilient mindset, allowing you to navigate life with grace and enthusiasm.

Embrace the present moment. Practice mindfulness and be fully present in each moment. Appreciate the beauty around you, the kindness of others, and the opportunities you have. This constant awareness of the present fosters a sense of joy and gratitude.

Cultivate a sense of curiosity. Approach life with a sense of wonder and exploration. Seek out new experiences, learn new skills, and embrace the unknown. This curiosity fosters a sense of growth and excitement, enriching your journey.

Celebrate small victories. Acknowledge and appreciate your achievements, no matter how small. Celebrate the progress you've made and the lessons you've learned. This practice of celebrating small victories fosters a sense of accomplishment and joy.

Embrace challenges as opportunities. Recognize that challenges and setbacks are part of the journey. Embrace them as opportunities for growth and learning. This positive perspective fosters resilience and a sense of adventure, allowing you to navigate life with grace and enthusiasm.

14

Chapter 14: Building a Support Network

A support network is essential for a balanced and fulfilling life. It provides the love, encouragement, and guidance we need to navigate life's challenges and celebrate its joys. Building a support network involves cultivating relationships that uplift and inspire you, fostering a sense of connection and community.

Identify the key people in your life. Reflect on the relationships that bring you joy, support, and inspiration. These are the individuals who form the foundation of your support network. Make an effort to nurture these relationships and express your appreciation for their presence in your life.

Reach out and connect. Make time to stay in touch with friends and family. Whether it's through regular phone calls, video chats, or in-person meetups, staying connected strengthens your bonds and enhances your relationships.

Seek out new connections. Engage in communities or groups that share your interests and values. Whether it's through hobbies, professional associations, or social events, these new connections broaden your support network and bring new perspectives into your life.

Be a supportive presence. Offer your support, encouragement, and love to the people in your life. By being a source of strength and inspiration for others, you create a positive and nurturing environment that fosters mutual growth and connection.

15

Chapter 15: The Practice of Self-Compassion

Self-compassion is the practice of treating yourself with the same kindness, understanding, and support that you would offer to a friend. It involves recognizing your worth and embracing your imperfections with empathy and acceptance. By practicing self-compassion, you cultivate a sense of inner peace and resilience.

Acknowledge your feelings and experiences. Allow yourself to feel and process your emotions without judgment. Recognize that it's okay to have moments of struggle and imperfection. This practice of self-awareness fosters a sense of acceptance and understanding.

Treat yourself with kindness. Speak to yourself with gentle and encouraging words. Offer yourself the same compassion and support that you would offer to a friend in need. This practice of self-kindness fosters a sense of self-worth and resilience.

Embrace your imperfections. Recognize that no one is perfect, and it's okay to make mistakes. Embrace your imperfections as part of your unique journey. This practice of self-acceptance fosters a sense of inner peace and confidence.

16

Chapter 16: Living with Intention

Living with intention is about aligning your actions with your values and goals. It involves making conscious choices that reflect your true self and purpose. By living with intention, you create a life that is meaningful, fulfilling, and in harmony with your aspirations.

Start by identifying your core values. Reflect on what matters most to you—whether it's family, creativity, health, or personal growth. These values serve as your guiding principles, helping you make decisions that align with your true self.

Set clear goals that reflect your values. Break them down into actionable steps and create a plan to achieve them. This intentional approach to goal-setting provides direction and motivation, empowering you to pursue your aspirations with confidence.

Make conscious choices in your daily life. From the activities you engage in to the people you surround yourself with, ensure that your choices reflect your values and support your goals. This practice of intentional living fosters a sense of purpose and fulfillment.

Reflect on your progress regularly. Take time to review your goals, celebrate your achievements, and adjust your plans as needed. This ongoing reflection ensures that you stay aligned with your values and continue to grow and evolve.

Book Description:

CHAPTER 16: LIVING WITH INTENTION

"The Rhythm of Enough: Daily Practices for Balance, Growth, and Meaningful Bonds" is a guide to living a life of harmony and fulfillment. Through seventeen chapters, the book explores practical strategies and mindful practices that foster balance, personal growth, and meaningful connections.

From creating morning rituals and embracing mindfulness to nourishing the body and cultivating a growth mindset, each chapter offers insights and actionable steps to enhance your well-being. The book delves into the art of building meaningful relationships, embracing simplicity, and practicing gratitude, providing a holistic approach to a balanced lifestyle.

With chapters on embracing creativity, finding joy in the journey, and living with intention, **"The Rhythm of Enough"** encourages readers to explore their passions and live authentically. Through a blend of practical advice, reflective exercises, and inspiring stories, the book empowers readers to navigate life's challenges with grace and resilience.

Whether you're seeking to enhance your personal well-being, build stronger relationships, or pursue your passions, **"The Rhythm of Enough"** offers a roadmap to a fulfilling and meaningful life.

This book is a testament to the power of intentional living and the beauty of finding balance in a world of constant change. Dive into its pages and discover the daily practices that will help you create a life of abundance, growth, and meaningful bonds.

www.ingramcontent.com/pod-product-compliance
Lightning Source LLC
LaVergne TN
LVHW020508080526
838202LV00057B/6243